THE SHUTTERED EYE

JULIA COPUS

The Shuttered Eye

BLOODAXE BOOKS

Bloodaxe Books Ltd acknowledges
the financial assistance of Northern Arts.

Cover printing by J. Thomson Colour Printers Ltd, Glasgow.

Printed in Great Britain by
Cromwell Press Ltd, Broughton Gifford, Melksham, Wiltshire.

çocukluk bir yemekti yedik bitti
(childhood was a meal; we ate it and it's finished)

WALL GRAFFITO, ISTANBUL

Acknowledgements

Acknowledgements are due to the editors of the following publications in which some of these poems first appeared: *The Bound Spiral, Envoi, Jersey Eisteddfod 1994 Competition Anthology, The North, Poetry London Newsletter, Poetry Review, The Rialto, The Spectator, A Squillet of Wise Fools' Gold* (National Autistic Society competition anthology, 1994), *Staple, Tabla, The Wide Skirt,* and *Writing Women.* Some were published in a pamphlet, *Walking in the Shadows* (Smith/Doorstop Books, 1995).

Thanks are due to South East Arts for a writer's bursary in 1993, and to the Society of Authors for an Eric Gregory Award in 1994. Some of these poems also won prizes in various poetry competitions, including several in 1994: Kitley Trust (a joint winner), Lincolnshire Literature Festival (first prize), Tabla (first prize), and The Poetry Business (joint winner).

I'd also like to thank Charles Barrow for the invaluable help and support he has given me in the preparation of this book.

Contents

Little Red-Cap

Mother, why have I come here? Is it
my destiny to wander this dark
forever, getting lost on the way?

Such tall trees; I cannot see
where they end, but their branches,
their hands, are rough-cast and careless

on my skin. At last now a little light is
filtering through the leaves. It draws me
like a root and by the time I emerge

I am a woman, stepping from the shadows.
Twigs snap at my feet; the forest closes
behind me. It feels my absence like a wound.

Orange

He comes back to a house
where the dark has splintered
in through every crack; broken
and entered. Inside, the clock ticks

loudly, like a heart in shock. Blood
bangs in his chest. He flicks on
lights, flings wide the doors on their
hinges like the orange jaws

of lions roaring to an empty night.
In the kitchen he pours himself out
a glass of home-made orange
wine and hovers by the telephone –

He calls their friends, neighbours, the police;
even the woman from the choral
society with the orange hair.
Everyone's out. Nobody's talking.

Several jars of wine later he
staggers to the window,
throws up the sash and bellows out
the names of his wife

and children. How different they sound
now, spinning into the night like strangers.
The night, also, is a tunnel speeding off:
no voices are heard. No voices.

It ends somewhere (he knows this)
with all the people who are suddenly
unattainable – neighbours, friends,
that orange-haired bitch – conferring

far off, out of earshot. He sinks down
onto the ruff-and-tumble rug where his
children used to play; buries his fingers
in the matted pile. His eyes glint green

through the gold liquid rocking
gently in its demi-john.
And by his head the black
phone hangs silent like the

shell of a foetus on its coiled
umbilicus, not moving.

Ellie's Vacation

They loaded the car with toys; Ellie's
wooden rocking-horse strapped
to the roof just would not be quiet.
The hostel had a name like a fairy-tale
but that was mostly a lie – except

there were witches all right:
mornings they served up fried
eggs at the hatch, the cooking fat
lying in pools on the dimpled
whites. The place was swarming

with lies: the toy-colours that
shouted at her to *Wake up!*
It's a dream – that's all! But Ellie
was in love, by then, with the mute
brandy-light of the real world falling

over everything just beyond the swell
of bay-windows in the entrance hall.
That summer her front tooth hung on
by the thinnest shred; her mother's
new friend started visiting,

told stories of cotton thread
looped round doorknobs: doors
slammed shut wrenching
tooth from bleeding gum.
And Ellie listened, crunching

on a big red fairy-tale
apple till her own tooth
sank into the spongy flesh and
stayed there like a polished seed shining
white among all the black ones.

The Back Seat of My Mother's Car

We left before I had time
to comfort you, to tell you that we nearly touched
hands in that vacuous half-dark. I wanted
to stem the burning waters running over me like tiny
rivers down my face and legs, but at the same time I was reaching out
for the slit in the window where the sky streamed in,
cold as ether, and I could see your fat mole-fingers grasping
the dusty August air. I pressed my face to the glass;
I was calling to you – *Daddy!* – as we screeched away into
the distance, my own hand tingling like an amputation.
You were mouthing something I still remember, the noiseless words
piercing me like that catgut shriek that flew up, furious as a sunset
pouring itself out against the sky. The ensuing silence
was the one clear thing I could decipher –
the roar of the engine drowning your voice,
with the cool slick glass between us.

With the cool slick glass between us,
the roar of the engine drowning, your voice
was the one clear thing I could decipher –
pouring itself out against the sky, the ensuing silence
piercing me like that catgut shriek that flew up, furious as a sunset.
You were mouthing something: I still remember the noiseless words,
the distance, my own hand tingling like an amputation.
I was calling to you, Daddy, as we screeched away into
the dusty August air. I pressed my face to the glass,
cold as ether, and I could see your fat mole-fingers grasping
for the slit in the window where the sky streamed in
rivers down my face and legs, but at the same time I was reaching out
to stem the burning waters running over me like tiny
hands in that vacuous half-dark. I wanted
to comfort you, to tell you that we nearly touched.
We left before I had time.

Afternoon Activities

Glass, said Miss Jenkins, is made of sand.
Her eyes glinted, mistress of a panoply
of facts that could dazzle, that tipped my whole
world casually off balance.
Furthermore, she offered, glass
is a liquid – like water. *It moves.*

I thought of the car-window and your voice
behind it; the way shock had made everything
suddenly mute; your face sealed behind
glass – under water – your astonished face
filling the frame; then the mad
swim of trees; telegraph poles
counting themselves out against
the soundtrack of a falling sky.

Later, in the sand-trough, I made my hands
disappear, or scooped up a fistful and
closed my fingers round it, keeping it in: the thrilled
darkness of a secret held like the frantic

burr of butterfly wings, and so powder-dry I
wanted to squeeze, to feel
again and again the small
collapse at the centre, like a sigh, and then

the steady pour of it: the shifting of sands,
the sound of a whole desert laughing.

Hansel's Dream

Believe me, little sister, I cannot show you
the path that brought us here: there is nothing
but berries on the forest floor. Hold out
your hand, Liebling – they are all
we have left. Take them and tell me,
what do you hear? Echoes, you say?
Echoes like the fall of an axe
hacking the trees to firewood?
Do not be taken in: it is only the wind
banging a withered limb against the bark.
This is truth, this coldness; this cold, wild dark.

Stop crying now. We must sleep till the moon
comes full in the sky and the shadows
move over us, soft as fingers. With my eyes
closed, I can see Salvation – a small,
low cottage with sweetmeat walls. I am tearing down
fists of bread from the roof, and you,
you are on tiptoe, trying the windows
with your tongue – a tentative lick, another,
until each little pane, brittle
as sugar cracks in your mouth, melts to a dark,
sweet mouthful of blood. At last,
I think, you are smiling.

Sister, we shall have a feast.

Pulling the Ivy

I

There was an avenue
of cedars all the way up

to the home where they
kept you because

your chest refused
to open itself out. It was

stubborn, they said, and you
looked up at me, grinning,

your small white face
all dimples, your bronchial

muscle clenched like a fist.
What I remember most

is the walls splashed
with primaries, bright

cartoon corridors that led
to your bed, and the smiles –

Mum, Dad and the nurses in the days
when we were all together still.

Or not quite apart. Outside
it was always Summer – rows

of lavender; I remember
the smell of it and its powder-soft

hue that would have come right
up over my head, except

I refused to stand next to it
to have my picture taken.

II

Dad got married yesterday.
At the ceremony

I wore ringlets, a green
ribbon and you helped

pull the ivy for my
bouquet, easing off

the tiny aerial rootlets,
one by one.

III

They joined hands, and through the image-
cluttered windows I saw the thick

velvet throats of the pasque-flowers
open for the sun: *all that I am*

I give to you. In the silence
they kept – which we all

kept – I heard you, for the first time,
breathing easily.

Digging the Pond

The colours have all
faded but the image

remains clear: three thin
shapeless bodies – me

in the middle with my hair
blown across my eyes,

squinting. On either side
my two brothers leaning

on spades and smiling,
faces and hands

muddied with clay.
We had built you

a pond – you had plans,
you said, to fill it with

200 rainbow trout.
Later, you took us back

to our *other house*
(the usual

scenes and tears)
and when we next phoned

the fish had all died from
sand in the gills;

an inability to
breathe underwater.

*

Photographs can do this.
It's like those quick

shifts of memory that come
out of nowhere: a split-

second buzz of
wings in my ear might

take me, for instance,
to that precise summer

day with the sound
of the weather suddenly

close to and a sky
full of crows barking

their importance – *Look! Look!* –
the glockenspiel chime

of an ice-cream van cruising
the empty streets with its

red-slick message – CAREFUL!
CHILDREN! – going quickly away.

The Letter

Just as I'm about to let go I freeze –
crisp vellum suspended. Below
the dark belly of the post-box.
Waiting. Certain of a result.

It is like the moments I've read about
just before death when a whole life whirrs
in your head, clack clack like old plastic
film re-coiling wildly onto its spools.

Last night I found a cross on a chain.
The intricacy of its silverwork
surprised me again, like when you pulled it out
from the space behind my left ear. Magic.

I was six; you sitting low on my playground wall
beside me. You'd come back, as promised,
your face still red from the blue, blue skies
of Malta, your red eyes enacting a smile.

No one else's Dad knew magic like that.
When the bell went I watched you disappear,
waved you smaller, till you were somewhere
out of sight beyond the gates. I stayed there,

watching still. And now it is the fear
of saying too much, or of saying not enough
that keeps me here, rooted by the post-box,
my clammy hand stuffed into its fixed grin.

Easter Reunion

There had been a mix-up with the robes –
the sacristan had sent the red for cleaning and so
you did the whole thing in purple. Luckily
the crowd was the usual muster of cataracts,
false teeth and resignation, and you, of course,
proceeded with characteristic aplomb.

You are reading a version of the Passion, your voice
pushing the message home in that terse,
speech-and-drama-school way. Not at all like a priest.
Not much like a father either. If I look up
our eyes will meet and too many questions
will need to be asked. Answered.
It was about 12 o'clock, you say,
when the sun stopped shining and darkness
covered the whole country, and the curtain
hanging in the temple was torn in two.

I'm sitting here, four, five rows back,
a woman now, with not so many ways
to reach you as there used to be; losing myself
in the service book, the smell of wood, the small ache
in the base of my spine. Then, hearing you turn
to bless the bread, the wine, I judge it safe
to raise my head – it is not so much the sanctity
of the act that moves me, but the sight
of that gold-spun cross stretched out
between your shoulder blades, the crack
of the tiny wafer in your hands. *This is my body...*
Do this in remembrance of me.

I leave you by the north door, safe in black and veiled
in perfunctory goodbyes, your hands simply
hanging, drained of blessings.

A Dream of Voices

I

In the dream of you blind
corridors wind down like
worm-holes underground.

Your voice surrounds me:
a wall my fingertips could
open to, touching

the rough grain of it. Sometimes
I stumble across an isolate
part of you – an eye perhaps

or your wide mouth, suspended,
as in the photograph that hung
in the halls of your radio station,

the glint of your tooth only
just visible – pure gold –
and that same voice booming

out into kitchens all along
the coastline, making old ladies
smile into their tea.

II

The odds of finding you here
are negligible. The first time
my mother sucked me from you

I foundered nine months till I grew
strong enough to push my way back
out to you; then lay there

gasping on the white bed.

III

In this black-flushed dream of you the corridors
are all leading nowhere no matter how fast

I go; I may never get you out again whole
but tonight in a dim-lit corner I discover

the child-me, aborted, still waiting to become
the person you would have made me.

I try speech but the sounds bounce off
the thick-stretched eyelid-skin that

covers it, pink-veined. It refuses to hear
the voice I have made – no more really than

the squeak of a cartwheel turning and not
the great rumbling of hooves you would have

taught me to speak with. Had I made it back to you.

Bluebeard's Wife

She woke to the hiss of rain, breathless
from the closeness of her dream – a room
strewn with aspects of herself like dolls
left out in the garden overnight,
and starred with the vacancy of eyes, the stench
of something animal. Possessive.

In the bathroom she contemplated herself
till the steam welled up and erased her,
clinging to the cold glass. Dressing quickly, she found
the murmur of a pulse behind her knees,
daubed herself with his favourite scent
to mask her smell; took care to lock the door.

By evening she had devised a recipe
for healing. She cooked by candlelight
in the fizz and spit of the kitchen,
felt her head fill with the fumes and heat
so that when the flames jumped she was startled
by the hulk of his frame in the doorway, backlit,
his mouth open like a wound, the smell of blood,
of tarnish; the key in his outstretched palm.

Portrait in Black and White

We are alone down here. The intimacy
of his fingers ought to bother me,
coaxing my hair, too gently, till it lies
down my back – like a river, he says.

The dark is cogent. I would be lost
without the calm of his voice explaining
the methods for expressing speed, the workings
of an iris diaphragm: how the leaves

open and close to take in varying degrees
of light. He pauses, steps back to admire
his handiwork, pretends not to notice me
colouring now. He is considering the effect

of light scatter in the negative, assessing
the circle of confusion. He tilts my head
a little to the left, pushes out a huge white
disc and positions it under my chin.

It hangs there like a planet; a private
moon opening the dark. He surveys me
cautiously through the lens, adjusts
perspective and depth of focus.

They should be ready Tuesday, he says:
it will take him that long to have me
hardened and fixed. I smile; the camera
opens its eye in alarm; the silver shifts

noiselessly into place.

The Smallest Room

School's out; a fine gauze-darkness settles
on the street like dust. She walks back alone,
feeling for the dampness of walls till they

open at her gate and she slips out of day
into another kind of chaos called home.
Violence bangs round her, stifles the sound of her

clicking the front door, then climbing the stairs.
Inside the magic of the smallest room she
watches the cold blue of the toilet bowl

vanish her unwrapped sandwiches, frothing
a while, then settling back to a flat
pooly silence. She stays there till the warmth of her

body sinks into the lino's gloss, head bent, fingers
reaching for that place far back inside her which
heaves her stomach into spasms and leaves her

trembling, pale, invincible.

The Last Days of Proverbia

6 am: the birds are out in force.
Worms are caught. High up on the hill
an ill wind is stirring; the tide
is rising fast. Bridges are built
and then crossed, with alarming speed.

Famine and floods are constant threats.
We spend the morning thinking up
ways to keep the wolves from the door:
our dogs have taken to sleeping
long hours, and we dare not wake them.

Lunch time: all the eggs are gathered
into a basket (several hatch
even before they are counted).
The milk is spilt and cried into,
and little good comes of it.

Giving up all hope of omelettes,
we make do with bread. For the men
it is not enough – the weakest
have started off towards the wall.
The change of scene will do them good.

Wary of strangers, we manage
to stall the doctor for a week
with the aid of seven apples.
But the wall is listening out;
sooner or later it will talk.

In view of our dwindling numbers
it is no longer safe to stay.
Reluctantly, we leave the dead
digging graves for one another
and set off in search of a fence.

Hepatitis A

She stayed there through the worst of it under
the gentle slope of the ceiling, felt the room
fill with dusk; the walls through a packed
mulch of straw and dung, breathing; fragrant.

He lay there moaning while his skin burned; deep
moans like the shifting of continents, a voice
she dared not recognise though she stayed
long after the doctor came diagnosing

hyperventilation in church due to a lack
of air. His skin grew slack, icteric;
she watched his features ebb into the lard
of his face till he was all but lost to her –

all but for the rolling of his eyes, the wild
iris-green that could not be dulled
while he still had strength enough to flinch
from the ice-water sponge she offered him.

Yards away in the street she hears the quiet
cars slicing a path through the dark with their wide
flat blades; each passing is like a sough of wind
that floods the room briefly and is gone:

all night and in no particular rhythm
they come. Persistent, like a slow strobe,
or the flush of his own sluggish pulse lit blue
under the pale translucence of his hands.

After, he praises her constancy – only
you should have let me cry out when I needed;
not tried to temper me. So ultimately she knows
she has failed; feels again whole empires slip

from her fingers, the hard scales fall from her eyes.

The Making of Eve

And kneeling one day at the sea's edge God
scooped a fist of mud from the earth and pressed it
into a shape called man. Its coldness spread

like an ache through his fingers and as He
stooped to warm them by chance a small
cloud of breath seeped into the shape and it lived.

But by and by when the sun was high up
in the sky man began to crack and fall
into pieces. Then God lifted some salt

water into his cupped hands and called it
woman, smoothing it into the fractured clay.
Now whenever man got hot he hankered for

a long cool sip from woman and she
assented sometimes wanting a place
to rest safe from the tireless assaults

of the wind and craving for a while
a different sort of medium to move in.

Proserpina's Lover

Like a slow fade-in, a scene emerging
from a screenful of black she appeared

one day under the drooping boughs of the orange
tree dripping with blossom. The sky sang blue;

flowers burst at her feet. Well, I know that kind
never hangs around for long, but the first time

she left the world turned mute; all the days ran
into each other like rain; birdsong stuck

in the little pulsing throats of birds, their bead-eyes
staring; vacant. A week later they were gone.

I crumbled, mouldered, longed for the warmth of her
willowy limbs. And then, when I was least

expecting it she returned, pouring words on me
till I melted and held her. Why can't it be

Summer forever? she asked. But her dreams
unsettled me: nestled in the cave of my arms

she would tremble, mumbling her lunatic stories
about the six seeds of a pomegranate – one

for every month she was with me, she said.
One for every month she was not. Each time

she returned she was a screen goddess stepping down
to the hush of her spellbound auditorium.

And each time I fell, believing she might
stay. Like a wave rolling shorewards and not leaving.

Darling, I would live and die in the snare
of your voice but you'll always be out of place
in a world that keeps on going, that will not
pause or play itself slow. You do not belong

in my world, love. So go.

Nutting

All summer we lived with the swollen heat,
barely touching except when, now and then,
the clouds, pregnant as cows, burst through the soft
caul of the sky to souse our dusty lungs.
One afternoon beneath the walnut tree,
I watched you biting into stiff green skin,
nose creasing as you spat the bitterness
off your tongue and, turning to me, revealed
the half-grown brain inside: *It's best,* you said,
to pick them now before the wooden husks
begin to form. So we worked on till dusk
filling our rucksacks to breaking point.

I found six jars in the cellar today:
nuts pickled black, blood-fat, baulking decay.

Homeopathy

A sixteenth-century Swiss alchemist
dabbled in the art

of healing like with like, observing that
the weaker the dose,

the stronger its curative properties.
I wonder: if I

ever so slightly stop loving you now
will you start to feel

the absence of me? How soon will a cure
be effected – and

what, would you say, is the likelihood of
a lasting result?

Miss Havisham's Letter

Darling, there is nothing between us that cannot be
restored. So much remains of the good times: did I tell you

how, on the eve of our day, while in my under-garments,
I leaned forward and felt the full weight of my breasts

in my own hands! And such pleasures have been replaced
by other pleasures – a kind of wisdom: my eye knows

the very corner of my eye, and my mouth has learned
to use its various muscles to full effect –

When my girl comes with food I pull a perfect scowl,
but I do not refuse the tasteless sops she brings:

how else shall I sustain myself! Darling, the dress
outgrew me long ago. I hear it sometimes

cracking in its paper where the silkworms
shift and slide. It is trying to make a life for itself.

And my small night table is shaping an effigy
of you; it sags with all the candles I have burned.

Pray God that you will be here soon; the furniture
is weary, my darling, of the names I am forever

fingering into its dust.

Masaccio's *Expulsion from Paradise*

I *Eve*

With one thumb extended he could eclipse the whole
naked length of her. He began to think of her face
beneath it; the dampness of clay; how it would feel
to smooth her small features to hollows. He imagined

his thumb pushing into the darkness of her
gaping mouth (if you lean in close you'll hear
the gargled moans lodged deep in her throat)
and once he'd smudged her eyes shut it was clear

she wouldn't want to open them again.
Her face is a mask; her hands like the hands of Venus
in the Pisa Duoma, concealing the sin
of nipple and vulva: *Shame,* they are saying, *Shame.*

II *Adam*

Like a convict emerging from court to the angry
flash of paparazzi he shields himself. *At which moment,*
he demands, *was I the richer – then, when I was hungry,
or now, being full? O there is a deep deep hole*

inside me and a chill wind stirs. He curls
his shoulders, steels himself, turning inwards, in-
coiled for the voice of God is always at his back.
And the shadows of his ribs, his fallen chin

lie like stigmata on his skin. Above his head,
in a world of muted parchment-browns, the Angel's
blood-skirts go flaming, and he lifts a maledictory sword,
feeling the stretch of his wing, the muscled length of it.

*

Woman holds herself straight, forcing her hurt face skywards.
And Man walks blind beside her, surveys himself through
the vast dark of his hands. They move as one but
separately now. Not looking. Not touching. Not wanting to.

The Marriage

Outside even the rain falling
was a kind of absence that slid

over everything the dark
afternoons contained –

the torn voices of dogs
barking out their squares

of territory, demanding
nothing beyond what was

rightfully theirs, and in the garden
a toppled plant pot half-

sunk where the earth had
grown up round it; so the sky

emptied itself now and hung
like a slackened muscle. And for him

there was nothing so comforting
as this very moment or others

just like it – a chair that nobody sat in
besides him, the touch of paper

under his fingers, pages
turned and milked and turned again.

And, in another room, nothing
so still as the pool of her eye,

her unblinking eye at the window,
watching the rain come down.

Don't Talk to Me About Fate

There are still nights I wake into darkness.
Dry-mouthed, unable to find myself.

And minutes later in the x-ray glare
of the kitchen, over-exposed, the migraine-

hum of the fridge, hogging its cool dark
like a secret. From here it's possible to see

the length of the landing rolling out
to a room at the end of it. An empty bed.

And the open door looking back at me,
slope-shouldered in silhouette, remembering

how easy it was then – how your teeth would fizz
for the tense thinness of a tequila glass, salt-

lipped, your tongue stiffening for the tang
of lime till your jaw ached. And later

your voice cracking a whisper: *it isn't
meant to be. I'm so sorry.* Don't talk to me

about fate. *I* meant it. But you will be sleeping now,
far off, unaware of how things go on

happening in the dark. Inches from your head,
for instance, an army of numbers forming

and re-forming themselves, liquid
crystals falling night-long silently into line.

What you hear is the flush of your own pulse.
Close by. Regular. Like a shuffling of cards.

one day my heart turned bad

one day my heart turned bad it was tired
of the whole routine the way I would
stand for days looking through the sooty
window of that bus say leaving you and you
not getting any smaller as you should

it was black bruised and raw it'd had enough
of meetings separations endlessly
leaving or being left so it built itself
a wall with windows so high nobody
could see in and it invited me

to stay well I was doubtful at first treading
the stony staircase cautious not daring to
look behind me at what I was again
leaving but o you should see the armoury
it has stored up there it wouldn't hesitate

I'm sure though so far I'm amazed
how quiet things are these days I can almost
hear what it's thinking and all in all
it seems best now just to sit tight and not
open the door to anyone

Maverick

A taxi from the airport and she's back
in the great Unknown unloading herself
from a suitcase – books she's read or plans

to read; some clothes, old letters, old doubts unfold.
And venturing outside what strikes her
is the greyness and again the colour

of flowers nodding from balconies; neighbours
hissing gossip from their high-up, high-rise
galleries: rubber necks and faces, painted

mouths swollen with intrigue, sensing a
hiatus in their trip-trap, orderly
going-nowhere lives. Words drop into

the air and burst, uncaught, in a language
she'll never master though the accompaniment's
the same – the bang of doors above and

below her, voices of children and outside
radios playing to this constant
building and re-building; the ring of metal

joints banged loose like the great dismantling
of a circus in the rain after
the final show, the leaving for the open road.

All These Miles

What can I tell you with all these miles pulled taut
between us and time split like fruit so everything

happens to me two whole hours before
it happens to you? Here, already, I can feel

the dumbstruck night disintegrate. Listen: it is
the hour of the dog – a thousand husk-throats hacking

a beach-long ache of sky. Beneath it someone
is walking me home, just inches from the quiet

shift and swell of the sea that takes us,
almost without sound, past the statue-white

chairs in the tea-garden crowding
the waterfront, facing seawards like ghosts.

My door is open; we climb into its shadow,
saying nothing, until only the moon is left

unchanged and familiar, and his face closer in, his
breathing like the sound of the whole sea in one, small

uninhabited shell; like the sighing of steam which starts
deep in the pistons, then shudders an engine into life.

The Sea-Polyp

Spineless and eyeless we spend our days
streaming circlets of tentacles
in the languid flow of the tide, effusing
grass skirts, snake-hair. To multiply we
simply divide; unknowingly and overnight
we lose a small part of ourselves
into the blueblack gloaming, deep and icily.

Often in clusters in clear deep pools
you will find us, gossamer-pink and clinging
to rocks as if we happened there: fleshy eruptions
on some dry pock-face, spreading our bases,
possessive, attached, and though we can't recreate
Medusa's stony stare, it is true that we paralyse with
the sinuous lengths of our hair; our elastic mouths
can accommodate creatures twice our size.

Lately I've been noticing, just a little
further down my rock, a new appendage – small,
bristling, perfectly formed, it has grown
a fine mouth-stalk and is relishing
independence, I think, but looks, by all accounts,
remarkably like me.

Cytogenetics

Parenthood is an art. We'll do it better do it
differently, we say, choosing to forget
that even flesh can be traced to the basic
stuff of plants. It's mapped out in the pin-prick

centre of each jellied cell: precisely how the lines
will gather, like plant-veins, on my skin;
how I'll fuck up in all the same ways; plug in
the hoover on turbo-boost and blast my children's

dreams into fragments just to make my presence felt.

Cut

The birth-screen is a canopy, hygienic
as sky. Its steel framework has her pinned

for part of an hour or a day; tubular,
gleaming cold. She feels herself finished before

they have even begun; again and again
the whiteness wipes her out. Somewhere

beyond it they are slicing a clean
wide smile: way down there beneath her

bikini line (so it won't show) she feels the knife
or the sensation of a knife going in

layer through layer till the bluish head
reveals itself like a bulb through the softly

glistening caul, rounded and perfectly formed.

Child

You would take the whole world into your mouth,
brick by coloured brick.

Tiny Sufi, truffle-pig, your hunger
frightens me; I must take care to fill
your little life with nugae, bright
primaries, and to wear my anxiety
lightly, like a shawl.

Daily the radio booms out
the atrocities I must keep you from:
the earth is diminishing by degrees,
we are eating more than we grow.

Small love, soon, soon you will recognise
the names of all these colours: blue
asbestos, green house – so many monuments to
our misguided ingenuity.

I should never have brought you here –
what milk is pure enough
to feed you with?

No hole, they say, no catacomb can
contain the clouds beneath our feet.

Breast

Already her body is no more
than an imprint on a spotlit

sheet, anaesthetised;
rootless. She's left it there,

gone off in search of
all the other bodies she has

lived in, growing back
fast into herself. And far off now

some place they can't
hear, she's heady with laughter

at the edge of a confident
nineteen, all the summer-long

nights melting round her.
Into her. By the time

daylight breaks on her
retina again she'll be

a blunt-limbed child lying
blameless on the high bed.

But this is not how it happens.
Light comes too soon; catches her

off guard so she tumbles
to earth and feels the grain

of cloth under her fingers:
a calm hand resting

flat against a bandaged chest.

The Wild Garden

All morning she fills the house
with music where her children used to be, the piano
singing out effortlessly under her
slim fingers. Later, through the feverish
eye of the kitchen window, its gloss-
paint curling in the frame, she looks out over
rows of gardens, hating the geometric
order of it all, the careful shapes of flower-beds,
the finely-hewn hedgerows. She goes out, gets
down on her knees in the scutch-grass, drawing out long,
rubber-white veins from the soil. The black
bags crackle for the mulch of weeds and leaves – her own
blood-waste slowing now, its blue adventures showing
in her hands like a map in 3D with rivers
here and here, a half-moon of dirt beneath
each fingernail. She has a bagful
of cuttings from places she has visited, and slowly,
slowly, she is filling the wasteland, piling up
memories, mixing desires in the damp
earth smells   oxlip, elder, a tangle of hemp-
nettles crowding the fence; hazel and red
bryony from her daughter's house.

She has an ear for music but cannot see
as clearly as she used to see, due to the uneven
geography of her eye.

Istanbul Dawn

Again this morning the memory of you
seeped through gauze-layers of dreams

the way the dawn lights bleed
into the Bosphorus or giant mosques

shoulder their way out of the mist at some
unearthly hour just to be certain

of a place in the skyline that's forming now
from this shapeless fog hanging damply

over a muscular sea.

The Tone-Poet

And here, he said, there are people dancing
in fields of barley. Can you see the gold
green ribbons streaming from their feet? Her hair

streamed like the sun. And the bleached stalks lay flat
under the sun, not moving. Do you feel it
on their faces; the way it bends to them? Listen.

When she fixed her eyes on me I was like dust
turning, turning in dry air, not certain
how or where to settle. So the people go on dancing

till the rain-clouds gather. It is a matter
of simple scoring – a flute pulls a bird from the air:
tweet, tweet. This is a storm; this the morning after.

Now I will show you what power there is
in the trumpet's slender throat; how it can
stop a heart from pulsing, cut clean through

the babbling, silvered sky. A trumpet
sounding its two-tone single message: *Listen...*
You know the rest, he said. And as he turns, the field

feels itself wide from shoulder to
shoulder, rolls its weary acres down,
down and on to the edge of the sky.

The sky absorbs itself; an empty hand
sinks deep in its pocket, empty
but for a pocket pencil, a sketch-

book full of birdsong. Behind him the birds
peck seeds from crushed barley sheaths. Tiny
drops of water drip silent from their husks.

The Shuttered Eye

One day she returned from the hospital
with photographs showing internal

scarring of upper lids, left and right. She slept
with one eye open, fixed on the insidious night.

Soon after, the weather changed: clouds blew in and
hung there, slowly at first, milk-white and dense,

and she responded, looking into herself, pondering
the nature of things – how, for instance,

she had watched her children surprise her, growing
into versions of themselves she had hardly dared

anticipate. They were far off now,
impossible to recover, though she plotted

their achievements and dreams as one might
chart the movements of the stars, and would go on

doing so when, at last, darkness came, velvet-
thick like the fall of a theatre curtain,

the shutting of an eyelid for the final time.

Courage

(i.m. Sylvia Plath)

It is winter; already your bones stiffen.

The days, bunched in the alleyway out back,
are holding a beauty of sorts, but the grasp
is rheumatic –
　　　　We're afraid to let go, they are saying.

This is no cellar, brimful
with dark invitation: for months now
you have been painting over the cracks, lovingly,
licking the walls till they gleamed and cried out –
　　　　See how far you have come!

The coal gas sinks
deep in the sump of your gut.
Only the rumble of the waterpipes is audible;
that and the thump, thump, thump of the attainable.

Another Country

I

But this is not the story you played me
night after night in our Stage House all those years

ago; the one which opens on your bloodshot eyes
screaming at me to *GetOutGetOut* because I had dared

to question. And then as if someone has
flicked on the bass boom I am breathing like a man

pursued but I'm frozen there, the hot blood-jet
loud in my ears. Camera zooms in from above

to me, my small body, like one of those shimmering
TV cartoons with no fixed outline that will not be

still and cannot be certain where they end or where
the rest of the world begins. Fear does that to you.

II

Outside, real feet slapping the pavement, my heart
going off like a drum. You came after me once.

– And knowing I would be seen the whole
length of the lamplit street I taught myself to cry

silently, hid in a shop doorway and watched you
pounding past; the spittle flying

from your lips, the words that found me
with radar precision as you blundered on,

words that hooked in my skin like
briars, or lodged somewhere deep

inside – bullets too dangerously
close to the heart to be moved.

III

So we sit drinking tea and talking as if
the past were another country whose ways

we have long forgotten. This is not
the story we used to know; we gauge our questions,

play the scene like pro's: your hand
on that bone-china plate isn't shaking.

And as I look up you smile, confident I won't
ever try that old flashback ruse again.

The Door

Here is a door. You know that
I am behind it for no other

reason than that you saw
me enter it, for you

will never be still
long enough to hear

the banging of my chest,
the voiceless fear that,

once inside, has nowhere
else to go. And if

the door has a lock
what then? For no lock

exists that cannot be
forced as you never

tire of reminding me.
Come for me, then, and tower

over me, let me
cower in your shadow,

put out the light,
for when I am no more

than a silhouette, backlit,
others will come tendering

rewards for my story.
And then I shall speak

but with an actor's voice,
going over every detail

slowly, in the wrong dialect.

Major Harwell Experiences Bliss

It only happened once – on a farm some miles north
of here. A slit trench, to give you the precise
location. Ten or so men and myself, crouching
in our flaccid skins. It was raining
cows and sheep, and we just couldn't seem to make sense
of the rhythms – the rootless limbs (thud), the bursts of white
hot shrapnel, the silences between the shells.

We were drowsy as insects, the smell of cordite
seeping into every pore, and overhead the high,
immaculate flame. If I look up I will see it –
blazing, untouchable, pure as ether
and white as the cocaine mountains of Peru.
Believe me: I have seen them. When I open my eyes
the ridge is behind me, and I'm riding
the air, caught on an updraught, my dusty wings
glistening as they beat, each possessing its own
Cyclopic eye. See, beneath the sway of grass,
and there, above the hedgerows, the silences
smile; they are comfortable here. Every now and then
I flick out a roll-mop tongue (I have developed
a certain taste for nectar) and I am
feeling my way into the irrepressible blue
of a cornflower when I find myself
back in the trench, amidst a rain of gunfire.

On questioning the Captain it transpired
that I had never left his side. Precisely how
the sensation was effected is also
a matter for debate – though some have suggested
the limbic structures of the temporal lobe
as a possible source.

January 6th, 1928

Was it the moon out west or the way
the whole of London melted overnight? For days
we had moved about in our city of glass,
treacherous and beautiful – we began to think
nothing of it. And what woke us in the end
was not the pounding on the door (which we took
in our bellies as we slept) but the stench
of sewage so strong we found ourselves
coughing our guts out into our eiderdowns.

Outside the streets were swimming, and now
I think of it – yes, the moon was spectacular
that night. We were up to our knees in it all the way
down Millbank to Horseferry Road and the road
whose name I forget where the voices screamed out
from the basements, so they say, although
by the time we arrived there was nothing
but water; water up to the railings and the bodies
nowhere to be seen.

The journey home was longer – heads down,
silent under the nervous flare
of gaslights, past the Tate where the oil-flat
slicks of the Landseers floated, twelve
swollen canvasses spilling their delirious
reds and greens over the Embankment walls.

You stopped then to tell me how it was before: how
the women were unloaded, screaming, from their boats
and frog-marched to the prison on the hill. Or were they
being loaded on? I never can remember that.

The Scream

The way is straight, say the flat-folk going about
their business in their long greatcoats. The air hardly
acknowledges them, they are so thin, and the road

streams under their booted feet – a rush of tarmac,
glistening, spectacular, though they do not see
the way the lights catch in it or the molten blue

twist of ocean just inches away with its mad
currents pulling in every direction. They do not look back
to where they've come from or to the blood-

hot screech of sky above their cut-paper heads.
They do not see me, appearing from nowhere,
as prophets do; little more than a ghost, a noiseless

shadow with my long fingers, my yellow skull-face,
the near-perfect O of my mouth. Slowly now
I form a tunnel with my hands to take my voice

far far out... I scream; the flat-folk do not
miss a step. Behind them the red sky seethes.

Bomb

A mother is calling to her children
far off beyond the Atlantic somewhere

to come home at once; it's getting dark –
and don't they know how much she needs them
with her now? It's very late; she mutters
a silent prayer, but her mind is playing tricks:
her lips close on the same names over and over like
fingers endlessly counting the rosary (she feels
her old faith restored to her). Last night she slept fitfully
on a make-shift bed in the local church.
The candles wept to see her lying there;
how the little flames leapt up, casting their monster shadows
on the walls: a litany of the living and the dead.
Names are chalked up daily like exam results;
the rescue-workers go on foraging
debris that is impossible to identify –
the wreckage of a fourth floor nursery littered with
the small limbs of dolls and children. All day they have searched
with their microphones, dogs, machines that can detect
the heat of a man's body through a solid wall
of rubble. On and on they go, burrowing, delving, probing.
Night spreads like fallout over the raging city.

Night spreads like fallout over the raging city
of rubble: on and on they go, burrowing, delving, probing
the heat of a man's body through a solid wall
with their microphones, dogs, machines that can detect
the small limbs of dolls and children. All day they have searched
the wreckage of a fourth floor nursery littered with
debris that is impossible to identify.
The rescue-workers go on foraging;
names are chalked up daily like exam results
on the walls: a litany of the living and the dead.
How the little flames leapt up, casting their monster shadows;
the candles wept to see her lying there
on a make-shift bed in the local church,
her old faith restored to her. Last night she slept fitfully,
fingers endlessly counting the rosary. She feels
her lips close on the same names over and over like
a silent prayer, but her mind is playing tricks
with her now. It's very late, she mutters –
and don't they know how much she needs them
to come home at once? It's getting dark;

far off beyond the Atlantic somewhere
a mother is calling to her children.

Passing By the Sirens

What stood out from the rest
was the whiteness of the shore
like the stretch of sheets, starch-white
on a guest-house bed; the calm
hush of waters and the words
I spat – *Every one a whore* –
over and over like a psalm.
But were they women or birds
those creatures who filled the night
air with voices drifting light
as zephyrs through the mist?

I stiffened; kept my spine pressed
to the mast, each note made more
real by the restraint, the bite
of those soft salt-kisses... warm
nights in Ithaca, the words
she breathed through my skin like words
from a creation myth: *white
is for death, love, her wings light
as your hands on my breast.*

Now the choir grew fainter at
the sight these words revealed – hulls
set at the sea's edge, the bleached
bones of sailors, their small skulls
grinning like maniacs far out
on the shore I never reached.

Old Man Sleeping

Behind his eyes the engine becomes
the low thrum of the womb, names
of stations distantly sounding

are like the lines he remembers
from fairy-tales – how the piper
led the children through a mesh of streets

to that mountainside door. So much dark,
and the drizzle soaking down all
evening along the track, the darkening sky.

Then waking to the hiss of pistons or is it
steam discharging to the quiet
opening of doors, sliding back into themselves.

Through the window dirt black
clouds gather an eclipse, invent
a land of sudden shadow

like stepping out onto a platform –
the slap of a shoe hitting tarmac
the moment the sky finally breaks.

The Botanical Artist

Today I am working on *Lactuca virosa* (that's
Bitter Lettuce to the uninformed). You will note
the raised lateral veins, the spikelets on the mid-
rib and the ear-like lobes which, I'll admit,
I have enlarged very slightly for effect.

Back in the sixties when I started, flowers
were my main concern. (You may have seen
my trumpet-burst of celandines on the sleeve
of *Freefall to Wonderland.*) I knew nothing then
of rhizomes and whorls or how the pistil
functioned, and the very mention
of roots left me cold – I just couldn't
get my mind around the wiry complications of those
leathery, leeching tongues beneath the soil.

These days, frankly, petals bore me. It's the mechanics
that matter: I can spend a whole morning
mixing my earth-reds, ochres and umbers
to reproduce the richness of a calyx, its lips
and teeth and the scales and hairy
folds of the throat. Now I dream
of roots and heart-shaped
clasping bases: one night I pulled
a mandrake from the ground – its scream
flew up like a blood-spurt, staining
the night-air, and the soul
went up after it, silently, furious.

Song of the Clock Girl

How old was I when I first
learnt how to tell time? Big hands

moving over little hands; little
hands in big. My father had a friend once who

took me flying, then wiped my mouth out, clean
as the birdless sky up here. Everywhere

I looked then there were doors to be locked; windows
which could not be covered, where thin

shards of light cut through to expose the still
beating heart of the house, found me

crouching in dark corners. Oh, but time
is a true friend, wiping the past from its

flat face, over and over. And you should hear
the music I make now, alone in my room, my own

dark, my wordless skull, ticking the minutes off
like a metronome; steadily, tick tock.

You should hear the echoes it makes.

Jonah

Some consolation this – washed up
on an off-shore island, besieged
by a glassy sky; the fierce red
glare of the sand, and the sun's bite
like salt on raw meat. It enters
into every corner, grinds in
under my nails. My fingerpads
burn with the memory of its touch.

It gets inside too. Take last night,
for instance. I dreamt I was back
in the womb: first the great, high vault
arching above me, then the suck
and pull as I half-slid, half-fell
in the gluey heat to that dark
dark chamber; the sting of juices
leeching my skin; my burning eyes.

But how did I come to be here?
I turn it over, trawl my mind
for images. There was a storm;
the boat was reefed. I remember
rough hands and the crash of the sea...
Then, out of the darkness, thunderous
light; the thrash of that mighty tail
retreating into still waters.

Spring Bank Holiday

The holiday season fizzles briefly
and is over. All the trees hold still
under a papery sky.

At four in the afternoon the sky dilates
with the chug, chug of petro-fog: tonight
the sun will set in technicolour.

The country feels itself shrinking
to the size of a map. All down its length the blue
roads are clotting now with the fitful pulse

of people in cars, hauling their impedimenta
in boxes and cases and haversacks back
to the night cheer of suburbia.

*

At midnight the last house shuts its yellow eye.
The shadow-folk have slid back into
their sheets and quilts. Outside, the forest

hums like an air-vent, breathing cyclically.

The Art of Interpretation

A plain wood table, the obligatory
vase of flowers, the writer's head bent low
over his work. At the far end, a window.

Open. Apart from this there is little
to help us with the story: the room is left
deliberately bare, inviting us

to speculate. Consider, for instance,
the window as eye. Is it looking out
or looking in? Notice, too, the dark, plum

sheen of the nib; and the pen, not poised
but resting, heavy, on the page. Unused.
Do you see how the artist plays the light

off against the shade? The candle, also,
is misleading: I advise you to ignore
the warmth of its glow. Drop the temperature

a little. Allow your eyes to wander
over the shadows, where the details are:
the clearly-labelled absinthe flask, half full,

half empty; the sweeping lines of the words
in the open letter, just visible
under the lifeless curl of his fingers.

Now turn up the volume of background noise,
the pub's detritus in the street outside.
Bring it level with the window. Then cut.